The New Youth Challenge

A Model for Working with Older Children
in School-Age Child Care

Steve Musson and Maurice Gibbons

School Age NOTES
P.O. Box 120674
Nashville, TN
U.S.A. 37212

Challenge Education Associates
3284 Tennyson Crescent
North Vancouver, B.C.
Canada   V7K 2A8

i

The New Youth Challenge

A Model for Working with Older Children in School-Age Child Care

Published in the U.S.A by:
School Age NOTES
P.O. Box 120674
Nashville, TN
U.S.A 37212

Published in Canada by:
Challenge Education Associates
3284 Tennyson Crescent,
North Vancouver, B.C.
Canada V7K 2A8

First Published in 1986
by Challenge Press.
Second Edition co-published by
School Age NOTES and
Challenge Education Associates.

Printed by BookCrafters,
Chelsea, Michigan.

Library of Congress
Catalogue Card Number: 88-62241

ISBN 0-917505-02-6

Acknowledgements

The authors would like to acknowledge the contributions
of the following persons and organizations:

The New Youth Challenge Team
Heather Kennedy
Kate Quenville
Randy Wallis
Bill Saul
who piloted many of these programs.

Barb Waterman (Coordinator, Spare Time Fun Centres)
who helped create the idea.

Elenor Wu & Hyne-Ju Cho
for preparing the manuscript.

Gwen Norman & Peter Norman
for designing the manual.

Canada Employment & Immigration Commission
Employment Development Branch
for funding the initial stages of this project.

Digitized images are from the pilot phase of the New Youth Challenge program except pages 48,
64, and 70 which are derived from photographs by David B. Sutton.

Table of Contents

Section I: What is the New Youth Challenge?   **1**

An Important Role to Play   3
A Vision for Youth Programs   6
A Model   7
What is Challenge?   9
Challenge-ability   10

Section II: How to Make the NYC Program Work   **13**

Patterns of Interaction   15
Beginning with Courses   20
Proceeding to Clubs   25
Advancing to Contracts   26
The Contractual Approach   30
Categories of Challenge   31
Shaping the Challenge   36
Brainstorming Possibilities with Kids   37

Section III: The Role of the Challenge Instructor   **41**

Instructor as Guide   43
Tools for the Instructor   47
The Tool Box Approach   47

Section IV: Practical Tools   **49**

Baselining: Focusing on Progress   51
Feedback   53
Goal-Setting for Youth Groups   56

Section V: Theoretical Tools   59

Frameworks for Motivation   61
Self-Esteem   68

Section VI: Proven Programs and Ideas   71

Adventure   73
Creative Expression   77
Sports   83
Practical Skills   87
Logical Inquiry   89
Community Service   93
Job Experience   97
Personal Improvement   101
More Ideas   103

A Final Word   105

About the Authors   106

Selected Bibliography   107

I: *What is the New Youth Challenge?*

An Important Role to Play

The field of child/youth care* is changing in many exciting ways. We are beginning to realize the impact we can have on the growth and development of young people. Afterschool programs of all types are becoming more sophisticated, more innovative. The New Youth Challenge (NYC) program represents a major step toward a vision of what quality child/youth care programs can become.

NYC programs teach new skills and attitudes to children in non-school settings. These programs empower children by giving them the wherewithal to direct their own actions and take responsibility for the activities that they are involved in. Encouraging children to direct their own programs is changing the face of contemporary child/youth care.

The idea of child-directed (or self-directed) programs is best accomplished through the medium of *challenge*. We define challenge as a systematic reaching forward, toward the difficult but valuable achievements that one desires. It is the drive to become the best one can be. Challenge is the pursuit of personal excellence.

* For our purposes, the child/youth care field encompasses the following organizations: daycares; school-aged child care facilities; teen groups; community centre programs; youth-at-risk programs; organized youth groups; extra-curricular school clubs, and; parents.
We group these 'organizations' together because they are all concerned with the child/youth (aged 7-17) and with *care*. To be sure, care for members of a teen group is different than, say, care for seven year olds in an School Age child care facility. But it is only a different aspect of the same thing - *care*. All are in the same business of promoting the personal development of children.

Our Role in the Development of Children

One of the cornerstones of the NYC approach is the belief that we, as child/youth care workers, can play a vital role in the personal development of children. We can possess a workable, compelling *vision* of where (or toward what) these children are developing. And we can use our programs as a vehicle to assist and enhance this natural development. We are not 'glorified babysitters' there simply to entertain and supervise children.

In this confusing age, nothing could be more important than teaching children how to challenge themselves, how to work toward a healthy sense of independence and how to direct their own lives. In our programs we can teach children to set their own goals and we can also teach them how to pursue those goals effectively. We can play a major role in a child's pursuit of his own excellence.

But this task is not without its pitfalls.

Obstacles to Child Development

In today's world children are faced with some major obstacles in their quest for personal development.

1) Urbanization and technology are depriving children of opportunities for natural play. Places to play are disappearing and ways of playing are changing radically.

2) Children are becoming over-programmed and passive because of the television they watch, the crowded schools they attend, over-structured recreation, and such electronic pastimes as computer and video games which may usurp human imagination.

3) The changing home environment; the rise of the single-parent family, the stresses of the two-career household, mothers entering the workforce while the children are still young, and the increasing incidence of open conflict and abuse in the home.

Now more than ever, children need to be shown how they can take control over their own actions and therefore over their own lives. They must learn how to challenge themselves so that they can deal effectively with an ever-changing world.

We Can Make a Difference

What follows is a manual that outlines a program powerful enough to accomplish many of child/youth care's loftiest goals. It is a program that begins at the child's own level, and guides him in working toward his own vision of personal excellence.

As child/youth care workers, we are in a unique position to help children grow. We can make a difference! Using the ideas expressed in this manual we can take a giant step forward.

A Vision for Youth Programs

You can't have a dream come true, until you have a dream.

Any quality youth program needs a vision. In order to be effective we require a clear picture of where we are going with our programs. We need to understand what it is we are trying to accomplish. In short, we need a vision, and a *map* that can show us how to get there.

A program vision can provide us with inspiration, direction, and a reference point for evaluation. Without a vision, programs are in constant danger of stalling or wandering off course. "If you do not know where you want to go, you will probably end up somewhere...else."

The New Youth Challenge program is a vision. At the same time it contains a map - a way to attain the vision.

The NYC vision culminates in the concept of the self-directed person. A self-directed person is one who is responsible, independent, and generally feels in control of his own life. He has learned how to set his own goals and to pursue them systematically and effectively. Children in after school programs can learn how to become self-directed. We, as caregivers/youth leaders can help them develop the necessary skills and attitudes.

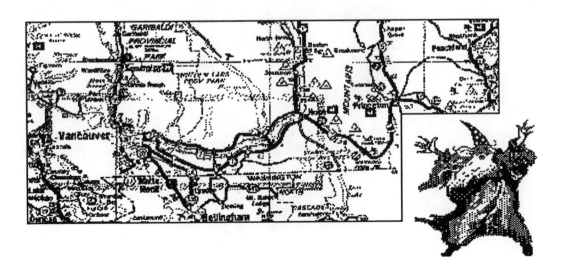

A Model

Directing one's own actions is not magic. It can be reduced to a simple series of learnable skills. The NYC program is structured to teach these skills in a logical, natural progression. The program involves three phases. (Figure I.1)

	PHASE 1	PHASE 2	PHASE 3
Theory	Expose participant to challenge activities	Give participant experience in challenging himself	Transfer owner-ship of challenge to participant
Organization	Instructor designed courses in challenge areas	Participant directed clubs in challenge areas	Individual participant contracts in challenge areas
Instruction	Direct instruction: Instructor selects and designs course	Shared instruction: Participants choose content & activities	Guidance: Individual sets goal and plans activities
Programs	eg. Course in backpacking skills	eg. Backpacking club plans a hiking trip	eg. Individual contracts for winter camping

Figure I.1: A Model of the Youth Care Challenge Program

Phase Three contains the vision of what young people can become within our programs. Phases One and Two represent steps toward the vision. Together, all three phases function as a map for youth programs. For without a map, our vision remains just a dream.

It is our belief that young people can learn to *direct their own programs*. Youth programs can be a place where young people actively answer the question, "What do we want to do?"

We feel that this vision of youth directing their own programs can best be reached through the medium of *challenge*. By learning what it takes to successfully meet a variety of challenges in different areas, young people can learn what it takes to meet any type of challenge. They develop their own 'challenge-ability': the skills necessary to deal effectively with an ever-changing world. We use activities in the areas of Adventure, Creative Expression, Sports, Practical Skills, Logical Inquiry, Job Experience and Personal Improvement to teach young people about the general *process of challenge*. Armed with the skills needed to effectively challenge themselves, they can begin to take control of their own lives. They can use our programs to direct their own personal development.

What is Challenge?

The word *challenge* implies much more than just excitement or thrill-seeking. And it is clearly not synonymous with words like danger or dare.

Challenge is the pursuit of personal goals. It is a reaching forward, an attempt to grow. It is the striving to attain new levels of performance that we set for ourselves.

Challenge is personal. Each individual carries around with him different ideas about what is challenging. A particular activity (such as rock-climbing or public-speaking) may be challenging to one person but not to another. And also, what is challenging to you now may not be challenging to you in five years. It all depends on 'where you are at' and what goals you set for yourself-- what new levels of performance you aspire to.

The notion of challenge, then, is closely related to the idea of goal-setting. If a person wants to achieve something (learn a new skill or accomplish a task) the pursuit of that goal is what constitutes a challenge.

The natural by-product of challenge is growth. The more a person successfully challenges himself, the greater will be his capacity to take on different and varied personal challenges in the future. The ability to challenge oneself is an integrated set of skills. And these skills can be learned.

Challenge-ability
Developing the Ability to Challenge Oneself

Challenge-ability can be defined as the desire and ability to challenge oneself. It is the ability to set personal goals and to work systematically to achieve them. It is the skill of aiming at, and attaining, those things that we desire in life.

A person can be said to possess a high level of challenge-ability if he continually strives to reach forward and become the very best he can be. It is the constant quest for personal excellence.

When we say personal excellence, we do not mean that everybody must become an Einstein, Ghandi, O.J. Simpson, or Mother Theresa. Personal excellence means being the best *you* that you can be. And make no mistake about it, that's challenging! In terms of a child, striving for personal excellence means putting out the effort required to be the best expression of himself that he can be. It does not mean that he has to be the smartest student in the class or the strongest kid on the block, just the very best at being himself.

The ability to challenge oneself is a valuable skill, especially in a fast-paced world where the only constant seems to be change itself. Challenge-ability can be used by the individual to take control of an ever-changing environment and to use change to help him grow.

The important thing to note about challenge-ability is that it can be learned. And if it can be learned, then it can also be built into our youth programs. How does one develop this ability in others?

There are two major components in the development of challenge-ability (in yourself and others). First, kids need EXPOSURE to challenging activities, EXPERIENCE with the phenomenon of challenge, and must then take OWNERSHIP for their challenges (Figure I.2).

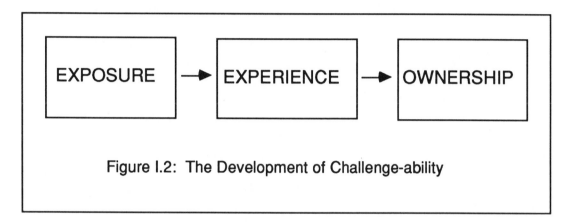

Figure I.2: The Development of Challenge-ability

Second, kids can learn about the *process of challenge*. They can learn to identify the common elements that go into a challenge of any sort. Techniques for goal-setting and systems for effective action can be mastered. Armed with these tools a child is better equiped to take ownership for his challenge activities. He can then direct his own quest for personal excellence, and begin to take control of his own life.

The main goal of New Youth Challenge programs is to develop a higher level of challenge-ability in each and every participant. We want each child to learn to desire challenge in their lives (as something constructive and positive), and we want each child to equip themselves with the techniques for effective goal attainment.

II: *How to Make the NYC Program Work*

Patterns of Interaction

The NYC program is based upon a simple, yet powerful series of interactive patterns. It is simple because it is built on logic and experience. It is powerful because it serves as a map for program progress and evaluation.

As we have said earlier, our vision is that of self-directed children pursuing personal goals within our programs. Well and good...but how do we get from *here* (where we are at now) to *there* (our vision)?

A major clue can be found in the patterns of interaction. That is, we can assess the development of a program by the type of interaction between the staff member and the participants. If we can determine the pattern of interaction that is most common between the staff member (hereafter called the Instructor) and the participants, then we can figure out how self-directing our participants are.

For example, if the Instructor is doing most, or all, of the talking, most of the planning, and most of the motivating, then our program is not very self-directed. On the other hand, if the bulk of program planning and motivation comes from the participants and the Instructor is used in a facilitating role, then the program can be classed as highly self-directed.

Directive Phase

The first interactive pattern we would expect to see in a youth program is one in which the bulk of communication flows *from the Instructor to the participants.*

This is quite a natural beginning for a youth program. After all, can we expect our participants to be self-directed right from the start?

This first phase we call *directive* because the Instructor takes on the bulk of program directing. We can use this phase to our advantage. Here we can concentrate on exposing our participants to well-run programs. They can see a quality program in operation. For if we expect them to direct their own programs in the near future they should get some exposure to well-run programs.

So our first interactive pattern looks like this:

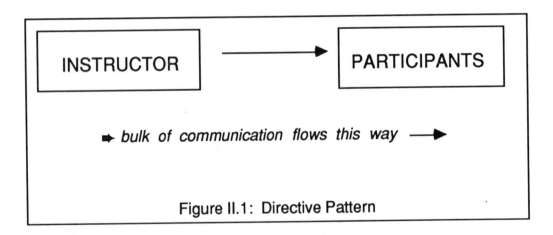

Figure II.1: Directive Pattern

This phase is equivalent to the Course phase outlined in Figure I.1.

Shared Influence Phase

Done effectively, the directive phase can quickly evolve into phase two. This phase is characterized by an even balance of communication between the Instructor and the participants. It is a two-way pattern. We call it the *shared influence* phase. In the first phase the participants were exposed to well-run programs. Now they can be expected to contribute significantly to the design and running of the programs. Using the skills developed in the first phase, the participants can now experience that which goes into a successful program. Under the supervision of the Instructor, they can experience what it is like to plan their own activities. This mutual influence phase is equivalent to the Club phase in Figure I.1. Diagramatically it looks like this:

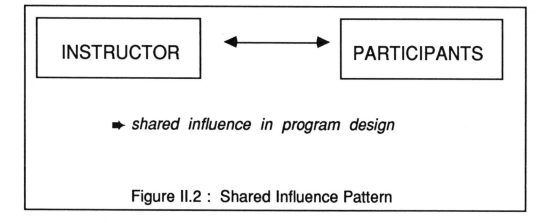

Figure II.2 : Shared Influence Pattern

Guidance Phase

In the final phase of the model we attain the vision we talked about earlier. The bulk of the communications at this stage originates from the participants. They are ready to take control of their own activities.

We are now in the realm of self-directed programming. The participants inform the Instructor what they want to do, and how they propose to do it. They have had *exposure* to well-run programs, and they have *experienced* what it is like to run their own programs. Now, in the third phase they are ready to accept full responsibility for their own activities. They have been properly prepared to take *ownership* of their programs. We call this the *guidance* phase, because the Instructor takes on the role of a guide, helping others to do what they want.

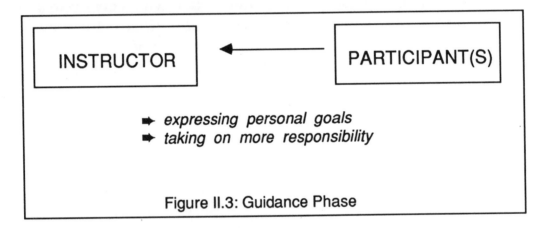

Figure II.3: Guidance Phase

This is equivalent to the Contract phase in Figure I.1.

Transfer to Living

The three interactive patterns represent a developing process of participant self-direction within the context of youth programs. If we could imagine a fourth phase it would involve the participants after they have left our programs. What do we want our participants to take with them when they leave? It could be called the *maturity* phase, represented by mature young adults creating their own goals and pursuing these goals for themselves. Or it could be called the *leadership* phase, where our well-trained participants seek leadership positions within our organization. It would look something like this:

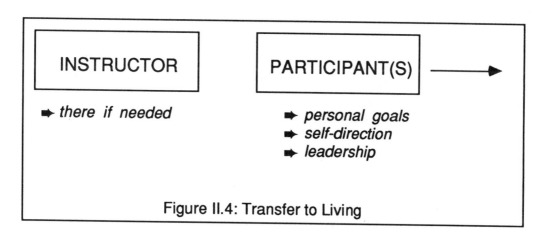

INSTRUCTOR	PARTICIPANT(S) →
➡ *there if needed*	➡ *personal goals* ➡ *self-direction* ➡ *leadership*

Figure II.4: Transfer to Living

An Important Note

Because of time or age limitations, not all youth organizations or groups will be able to get their programs to the more advanced interactive patterns. Some young people may not be ready, some organizations may not have the resources.

The important point to note is that we can all work toward these later phases. We may not accomplish the entire process, but we can use these later phases as a vision. These later phases serve to give direction to the earlier phases. We may not be able to move all the way to the end of the process, but we can all *move forward!*

The next sections of this manual show you how to incorporate these interactive patterns into your child/youth program.

Beginning with Courses

Consistent with our patterns of interaction, the NYC program begins with relatively structured experiences we call *challenge courses*. In these courses the bulk of the program design and execution is done by the Instructor.

In terms of ultimate vision of young people directing their own programs, it is our belief (and our experience) that kids need to be *exposed* to well-run programs before they can realistically be expected to direct their own. They need to see what a program looks like before they can be expected to replicate it under their own stewardship.

Challenge courses are an important beginning in the whole challenge process. It is here that the kids can pick up valuable skills in a formal teaching/learning setting. It is also here, in the structured courses, that the kids can be exposed to various ideas of what they can become. Skill-oriented courses such as First Aid, Wilderness Survival, Carpentry, Cooking and Babysitting fit in well here.

A series of successful courses will naturally lead to the children suggesting other topics that they are interested in. Of a well-run challenge course they will exclaim, "That was great, what's next?".

How to Design a Challenge Course

Step 1: *The Challenge Event*

The design of a course begins by setting a *challenge event*. This event represents an attainable vision of group excellence. It should contain various powerful, beckoning images that appeal to each individuals' desire for achievement and personal challenge.

Here are a few guidelines to use when designing a challenge event:

1) The level of challenge inherent in the challenge event should be sufficiently high to sustain motivation throughout the entire process, but it must be realistic and, above all, attainable.

2) It must be attainable by all participants *in principle*; that is, given a good dose of hard work and commitment. The success of the challenge event should never be *guaranteed* in advance.

3) The challenge event must be based upon the Instructor's evaluation of the group's readiness. He must take into account each participant's skills, resources and time.

And finally,

4) Some input from potential participants may be required in order to find some activity areas that would be of interest to your target population.

The Challenge Event:

> **A POWERFUL,
> ATTAINABLE VISION
> OF GROUP EXCELLENCE**

Step 2: *Study Units*

Once a challenge event has been specified the next thing for the Instuctor to do is to decide upon the first steps needed to attain the vision. He must ask himself "What do the kids need to know/learn in order to successfully meet this challenge?".

The content of these study units can be divided into skills, knowledge and attitudes.

Usually the teaching of skills is more readily accepted by young people in a course setting. A good principle to follow when teaching these courses is *keep it simple*. Always relate the learning that is happening to the attainment of the vision. The *relationship of learning to challenge* is an important one. It is a good idea when the course meets for the first time to show the children the whole program design. In this way they can make the all-important connection between study/skill development/effort and a challenge successfully met.

The Study Units:

Skills	Knowledge	Attitudes	Skills

Step 3: *Practical Units*

Practical units represent the intermediate step between the study units and the challenge event. The content of these units can be determined by the answer to the question "In what situations could the children practice and test the skills that they learned in the study units?" The content of these units could also be determined by figuring out what practical experiences are required before the participants could be deemed ready to accept the final challenge event. These units can take such forms as field trips, tours or mini-challenges. They can also be thought of as sub-goals on the road to the final goal.

Practical Units:

Practising skills that were learned in study units.

Final preparation before attempting the challenge event.

The key to a well-designed challenge course lies in a smooth progression from study units to practical units to the challenge event. This progressive learning design allows participants to accept the final challenge event as a *challenge*, and not as a threat, dare, or a meaningless adventure.

Course Design: *Putting it all Together*

Here is what a challenge course looks like once all the steps have been taken:

CHALLENGE EVENT

Vision of Group Excellence

PRACTICAL UNITS

Practising skills that were learned in study units.

Final preparation before attempting the challenge event.

STUDY UNITS

Skills	Knowledge	Attitudes	Skills

A blank form to use for designing your own challenge programs is provided on the next page.

Challenge
Event

Practical
Units

Study
Units

Lesson
Plans

Challenge Category:

Designer:

Proceeding to Clubs

In the challenge courses the participants are *exposed* to quality programs. In challenge clubs the participants *experience* their own challenges under guided supervision. This is consistent with the shared influence phase of Instructor/Participant interaction.

The progression from courses to clubs is a natural one. Once kids develop a number of skills they naturally want to put these to the test. A success in one or two courses will lead kids to seek more challenges and then more control over those challenges.

For example, when a group has been exposed to a series of challenge courses involving say, hiking, survival and camping, it is quite likely that they would form a outdoor club with a view to planning their own backpacking trip with some help from the Instructor. Or a group that has been exposed to courses in dance or drama may decide to make a Rock Video.

Once a club decides what it wants to do, it is a good idea to use the same format used in the courses (i.e., challenge event, study units, practical units). This allows the kids to replicate the process that they were exposed to in the courses. The important difference now is that they are starting to direct their own experience. They are beginning to take control of their own programs.

It should be noted that these clubs still require a lot of supervision. In the courses, the Instructor was the leader. Now the kids must learn to lead themselves. The Instructor's role shifts from a content-oriented teacher (as in a First-Aid course) to a process-oriented facilitator. Process orientation focuses on things like group management, effective action plans and problem-solving. All of these process-skills are directly related to the development of challenge-ability in each participant.

For a youth group/centre, this club phase can be an incredibly exciting time. Young people begin to use our programs to further their own personal development. The facilities and talents of our organization begin to be used to express the real desires of our clients.

We can also begin to prepare the ground for the next phase in self-directed programs, the contract phase.

Advancing to Contracts

If everything has gone well up to this point for the individual (or group), the *action contract* is a natural progression from courses and clubs. Up to now the challenges have taken place within the comfort and security of a peer group setting. Now it is time for the individual participant to strike out on his own, to pursue his own goals and to take personal *ownership* of his challenge activities.

An action contract is a powerful tool for anyone, but it is even more effective when it is offered to the individual after he has learned the basics through challenge courses and clubs. The action contract represents the ultimate in self-direction within the context of youth programs. It is our last chance to empower young people before they leave our organization as mature young adults.

In terms of our interactive phases, individuals within the program would tell the Instructor *what* they want and *how* they plan to do it, thus taking on the lion's share of responsibility for the way they spend their time in our programs.

The role of the Instructor is relegated to an advice-giver, resource person and/or systems-checker.

What is an Action Contract?

An action contract is a way for an individual to mobilize the power of systematic action in the pursuit of a personal goal. As a *contract*, it is a promise made to oneself to get out and do what you want. As a *system*, the action contract represents a very effective way to focus effort to achieve a personal goal.

An action contract is made up of five sections:

- Goal
- Plan
- Management
- Results
- Renewal

Action CONTRACT

Name:	Start Date:
	Completion Date:

Goal:

Plan:

Management:

Results:

Renewal:

Goal:
- a goal is a vision of some aspect of personal excellence.
- it should be stated in operational (workable) terms, and should be:
  - important to you
  - worthy of effort
  - attainable
  - measureable

Plan:
- a plan describes what you must do in order to reach your goals.
- planning means deciding on all that you need to ensure success, and the best order in which to do it all.
- includes; options, strategies and priorities.

Management:
- after you make a plan, then you must *manage* it.
- management means putting your plan into *action*.
- concentrate on making action *effective*, keep activity on track.
- includes; baselining, motivation techniques, charting progress, contacts, timelines and scheduling.

Results:
- results refer to outcomes you expect at the end of the contract process. But these results can (and should) be specified *before* you start your contract! You must be able to decide *ahead of time* how you are going to judge your results.
- you must set out criteria for your future success.
- specify minimum results, satisfactory results, and performances of personal excellence.

Renewal:
- this section can be filled out at the end of the contract process.
- It represents two things:
  1) Looking back - What did I learn?...about activity, the challenge process, myself?
  2) Looking ahead - What next? How can I challenge myself next?

The Contractual Approach

The action contract is the culmination of the New Youth Challenge program. And the *contractual approach* is also the cornerstone of the overall program design.

A contractual approach simply means that there is a shared accountability for the success of NYC programs. The success of these programs do not lie solely in the lap of the staff members.

 In challenge courses the participants buy into the challenge event. It is something that they *want to do*, and is therefore something that they must accept some responsibility for. In challenge clubs the kids begin to design their own programs and therefore accept a lot of the responsibility for their successes (and failures).

And finally, in the action contract the responsibility for success lies squarely upon the shoulders of the contractor. Raising the levels of responsibility as each stage of the challenge process is mastered allows the individual to enter the world of adulthood with a healthy attitude toward the idea of being responsible for one's experiences.

The Categories of Challenge

The New Youth Challenge program is divided into eight categories of challenge; adventure, creative expression, sports, practical skills, logical inquiry, community service, job experience, and personal improvement. The purpose of these categories is to assist the Instructors and participants in developing ideas for courses, clubs and contracts.

Each category is defined below, and examples are given. Each activity is divided into a *topic* and a specific *challenge*. The challenge must be stated in performance terms because the topic is usually non-operational.

Here are the challenge categories:

Adventure

 A challenge that involves a testing of the child(ren)'s personal competence and confidence in an unfamiliar environment. Adventure challenges are often physical in nature, but can also be personal, psychological or social.

Examples :

TOPIC ....CHALLENGE (in performance terms)

Backpacking.....................organize a 3 day backpacking trip

Bicycle touring ....go on a 3 day cycle trip

Rock-climbing ....master a one pitch top-rope and rappell

Farm life ....spend 3 days working as a farm-hand

Creative Expression

A challenge to explore, cultivate and express the child(ren)'s own imagination. Creative challenges involve both learning about the creative arts, and participating in the process of expressing creativity.

Examples

TOPIC ....CHALLENGE (in performance terms)

Drama ....write and produce a one-act play

Rock Video ....produce a rock video from scratch

Japanese Art.....................learn about Japanese art forms
                                                        through classroom activities and practice

Sports

A challenge that involves the pursuit of personal athletic excellence through competitive games, cooperative ventures or individual effort.

Examples

TOPIC ....CHALLENGE (in performance terms)

Soccer ....put on an invitational soccer tournament

Gymnastics ....put on a gymnastics display for school
                                                        or make the city championships

Baseball ....produce the best possible team we can:
                                                        play a league team

Practical Skills

A challenge to explore a basic skill useful in everyday living. Creating something useful or exhibiting a skill with practical real-life application.

Examples

TOPIC ....CHALLENGE (in performance terms)

First Aid.............................acquire an emergency first aid certificate

Self-Defence ....earn a yellow-belt karate

Bicycle maintenance ....strip, clean and rebuild an old bicycle

Cooking ....cook 7 different dinners in one week

Logical Inquiry

A challenge to explore one's curiosity, to gain a fuller understanding of a phenomenon that is of particular interest to the child(ren).

Examples

TOPIC ....CHALLENGE (in performance terms)

Astronomy ....learn 7 constellations; locate them on a
           clear night

Chess ....learn grandmaster strategies;
           organize a tournament

Weather ....foretell local weather over a week period

Community Service

A challenge to help your community through volunteering a service. To learn about the needs of your community and about your power to assist in meeting those needs through volunteer work.

Examples

TOPIC ....CHALLENGE (in performance terms)

Senior Citizens ....produce a show to entertain at
                                  Senior centres

Teens in Trouble ....create a peer counselling team

Hospitals ....volunteer and work as a candy-striper

Job Experience

A challenge to become job-ready for the local labour market. To gain the skill, experience and references needed to open the door to a first time job. Job experience challenges can also be fund-raising work projects for youth groups.

Examples

TOPIC ....CHALLENGE (in performance terms)

Landscaping ....operate a small lawn-cutting business

Daycare............................volunteer at a local day-care centre

Salesmanship...................organize a group fund-raising sale

Resume ....learn to write effective resumes

Personal Improvement

A challenge to change something about yourself that you feel you want to change for the better. To improve some aspect of your body, mind, or personality through commitment and hard work.

Examples

TOPIC ....CHALLENGE (in performance terms)

Weight control ....design a nutrition/fitness plan

Fitness ....attain a pre-set fitness level

Homework ....develop a program to improve
　　　　　　　　　　　　academic record

Shaping the Challenge

Ideas for challenge courses, clubs or contracts can come from anyone. Almost any activity can be made into a challenge. However, a problem that an Instructor might encounter in putting a program down on paper is the tendency to confuse a *topic* with a challenge event.

A topic could be backpacking, dance or cooking. But strictly speaking, these are not yet challenges. A challenge event must specify an expected performance level. It must give us insight into *how* the group (or individual) will be challenged and at what level they will be expected to perform to meet this challenge. Nobody's challenge is *backpacking* or *dancing* -- it is a particular performance level within one of those topics. The challenge event must be measureable.

An effective way to translate a topic into a challenge event is to:

1) Specify a performance level based upon the group's present abilities.
2) Specify concrete goal-attainment indicators.
3) Specify a time limit. Performance levels must be attained by a certain time. Put steps toward the challenge event on a time line.
4) Specify any special conditions: limits to outside help, quality of group interaction, sportsmanship and cooperation, or other factors.

This process of shaping the challenge has several advantages.

1) It creates realistic expectations for all group members.
2) It provides a standard for evaluation ("we did better then we thought" or "we got half way").
3) It is an easy step to move from a well-articulated challenge event to the initial stages of program planning.

One final word about shaping challenge events: beware of statements that imply all-or-nothing. There are situations, such as sports challenges, where it is better to speak in terms of *effort* or *trying* rather than *winning* or *conquering*. For if it is an all-or-nothing situation and the group does not win, then they might feel that the whole challenge, and all the effort that went into it, was a failure. But there is no failure in trying, only in not trying.

Brainstorming Possibilities with Kids

Who knows what is best for kids?

Who should decide what kids *want* to do? The most effective answer is the kids themselves! Given the necessary exposure and experience, they can decide what is best for them in the context of our (their) programs. As youth care workers, the best course of action we can take is to *ask* the kids how they want to spend their time in our programs.

Obviously kids can be misled as to what they want to do. They can be unduly influenced by current trends, the media or peers. But remember that, under all those outside forces, a kid is a kid. By their very nature, young people *need* to challenge themselves. They need to find out *who they are*.

The most effective way to find out what kids want to do is to ask them directly, "What do you want to do (in this program or organization)?". But this question is not as simple as it first might appear. Many young people cannot understand the scope of the question. Others cannot formulate a coherent, meaningful answer to the question. (Many adults have real problems with this question too.)

You may have to structure the question somewhat. Certainly a discussion of your organization's mandate (i.e., what your organization is all about, the purpose of your job, etc.) might be helpful. An inventory of the resources available, and their limits would also be helpful. This is not meant to limit input, but rather to put the question, "What do you want to do?" into context and

 therefore make it easier to understand. The kids may also need a place to start. We have found that breaking down the myriad of possibilities into the eight different challenge categories is very helpful in this process.

Outlining each category will undoubtedly give the kids a lot of ideas. Examples of activities in each category can be helpful, but be careful not to unduly influence their subsequent suggestions.

From here a brainstorming session with the kids is usually the most effective way to proceed.

Here are four simple rules for brainstorming possibilities with kids (adapted form Sidney Simon et al. *Values Clarification*).

1) Do not evaluate suggestions during the brainstorming session itself. This tends to make people defensive and interferes with creativity.

2) Everyone should be encouraged to think up as wild a suggestion as possible. It is easier to tame down a wild idea than to spike up a bland one.

3) Encourage quantity. The more ideas the better the chance that a good one will pop up. Every group member should be encouraged to participate.

4) Everyone should attempt to build upon or modify the ideas of others. Combining or modifying suggestions can lead to really unique and creative ideas.

For example, during a series of fast and furious brainstorming sessions, we received the following original and unique ideas:
• Ice soccer
• Teens producing a community service commercial
• Twenty man full-contact racquetball
• Jello-wrestling for kids
• Buy an old Arctic icebreaker and attempt the Northwest Passage

Some of these ideas may have to be modified (maybe), but each one contains the seeds of powerful possibilities. Kids are the best source of ideas about how they want to spend their time. It is our belief that it is best to get the kids to do what they want to do, rather that what *we think* they *should* want to do. This is not always an easy objective to accomplish (although it is easier than most people think). This is our challenge as creative youth care workers.

III: *The Role of the Challenge Instructor*

Instructor as Guide

We call the staff member involved in the NYC program an *Instructor*. Of course he does a lot more than instruct. He specializes in creating learning situations. Children never stop learning. If an Instructor is good, then the children surrounding him will learn even when he is not instructing.

In terms of direct instruction, the Instructor is expected to have a good grasp of two important things:
1) The *content* of the course, club, or contract material.
2) The challenge *process*, namely; visions, goal-setting, planning, management, evaluation, renewal, and the attendant techniques.

This manual represents a major step toward developing these two conditions.

The Challenge Instructor's role is analogous to the role of a mountain guide. We use the guide analogy because, just as a mountain guide does not carry his clients to the top of the mountain on his back, an instructor cannot be expected to carry his participants through their own learning and development experiences.

Being a guide means perfecting the art of allowing people to discover things on their own. In terms of personal development, a guide creates situations for its expression but does not demand this expression.

Like a mountain guide, an Instructor must know how to get the best effort out of each individual involved.

And both guide and Instructor work to help their clients gain the skills and experience necessary for them to go out and do it on their own. A good guide will work himself out of a job; he will teach so well that his clients can go out and climb their own mountains, meet their own challenges.

As Instructors we can use our adult knowledge and experience to allow our participants to learn and discover what they want. And over time we can help them *learn how to learn* and discover on their own. A good guide/Instructor is one whose group , upon successfully meeting a challenge, exclaims together "There, we did it ourselves!"

As Instructors we are in a position to have a great (but not exclusive) impact upon teaching/learning situations. The primary goal of these situations is to increase each participant's sense of personal competence and confidence. No learning can take place unless the learner possesses these.

A learner must *feel* that he is competent enough to master a skill. He must also feel confident enough to reach forward and trust himself to learn. This would suggest that we make sure these conditions exist in our teaching/learning situations or prior to these situations. If you could only teach your participants one thing, teach them that they *can* learn. All other learning is built upon this belief. It should always be included in your lessons.

Teaching for Success

In NYC programs, the child is the curriculum. After all, we are not really teaching rock-climbing, dance, or cooking, we are really teaching *children*. Their personal development is the standard by which we can evaluate our own teaching. We must adopt the approach of teaching for success. Like guides, we have a vested interest in our students succeeding. Their achievements are our achievements.

What we teach them in NYC programs is not as important as the fact that they are developing and maturing through our teaching (and through their learning).

Although program content should not be compromised, the main determinant in any teaching/learning situation should be the personal development of the individual child. This principle becomes more and more important as the program progresses from courses to clubs to contracts. For at the end of an NYC program, we do not want a child who is merely stuffed with knowledge and skills. We want to see a child who has learned how to learn.

A good Instuctor will make it a practice to check that content-learning is happening in his group. However, it is even more important to assess whether or not growth and development are taking place. The Instructor should ask himself:

1) Are they learning *how* to learn?
2) Are they *taking control* of their own learning experiences?
3) Are they taking *responsibility* for their own learning?
4) Do they see themselves as becoming more *competent?*
5) Are they gaining a sense of *confidence?*

It is important that our programs help our participants create a winning feeling. To a certain extent that winning feeling is structured in the course phase. There is a place for badges, rewards and certificates here. As the program progresses into clubs and contracts, the responsibility for creating that winning feeling falls more and more on the shoulders of the participants themselves.

One final word about the Instructor's role as guide. As with a mountain guide, one of the primary objectives of Instructors has to be the safety of his charges. It must be recognized that safety is an implicit objective in any *journey*. In our programs, safety must take primacy. Safety, as a subject, should be taught in all NYC programs. Safety techniques and attitudes can be incorporated into the study units and practiced throughout the entire challenge program.

The role of the Instructor is indeed a complex one. The Instuctor must be many things to many people. He must be in control at all times, and yet let others take control when they are ready (although these two types of control are not mutually exclusive). It is the purpose of this manual to assist the Challenge Instructor in meeting the demands of this complex but exciting role.

Tools for the Instructor

In New Youth Challenge programs, there can be no set or inflexible 'how to'. To really be effective, the Instructor must have a lot of room to use or express his own style.

An instructor can create, within his students, a desire to learn. This comes easily when the following conditions are met:

1) The students have *real input* into the challenge vision and into the steps necessary to attain that vision.
2) The students feel that they are truly *discovering* the knowledge, skills, and attitudes for themselves.
3) The students are allowed to see the learning process that they are involved in. They should be encouraged to *take control* of that process when they are ready.
4) The Instructor should allow for a maximum of *learner- directed* activities to take place. As Fritz Perls once said, "Only what we discover ourselves is truly learned".
5) The Instructor should possess (and show) a real *sense of wonder* with regard to both content and process.

We must work hard to create an atmosphere wherein learning is experienced as personal and relevent. We want to produce a situation where the child asks of the Instuctor "Please help me do it myself".

The Tool-Box Approach

The Instructor could look at his role much like that of a skilled tradesman. No two people problems are ever really the same - just as no two construction problems that require a skilled tradesman are exactly the same. No single approach will be effective in all situations. We recommend that the 'challenge tradesman' get himself a tool box. This tool box can be filled with useful tools that can be applied to problems (opportunities) as the Instructor sees fit.

The advantage of this approach is that it allows the Instructor to learn from others (borrow tools from them) while still relying on his own experience and judgement to decide when, how and where to use them.

Some tools are practical and some are theoretical. Practical tools are usually structured ways of communicating or interacting with children. Theoretical tools are primarily ways of looking at things or situations. These two types of tools are complementary. Here are some tools to start to fill your tool box.

Feel free to add others to your tool box as you see fit. (Hint: Looking at your own style probably holds a wealth of powerful tools).

IV: *Practical Tools*

Baselining: Focusing on Progress

Baselining is a practical tool that helps kids link their present efforts to their challenge goals. A baseline is a concrete measurement of a group's (or an individual's) performance ability before they embark upon a challenge project. It expresses how much the group knows about the field in which it has chosen to challenge itself, and how well it performs in it *now*, before they begin to work on the challenge. A baseline represents the group's starting point, described as precisely as possible.

For example, before beginning lessons for a dance program, an Instructor could video-tape the current level(s) of dancing skills possessed by the participants. This video-tape could be shown to

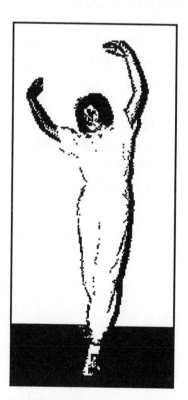

the group once or twice in the following weeks (while the group is busy learning), and also at the end of the program to show their progress. Different challenges require different kinds of baselining techniques.

The purpose of baselining is not to intimidate people with what they do not know, it is to help them get a sense of *progress thoughout the program.* A baseline measurement should be repeatable throughout the program and especially at the end of the program. The baseline and subsequent progress becomes the measure of a group's success. It could be up to the group members themselves to devise an appropriate measurement that could be used to compare where they started to where they finished.

A baseline measurement can be a powerful motivator. When a group is able to focus on its progress from baseline, it can see how far it has progressed and will be motivated to continue to improve. Nothing succeeds like success. Just knowing that the measurement will be repeated throughout the program will motivate kids to improve.

Without a baseline measurement we can easily forget where we started, thus we can become frustrated with our apparent lack of success. If we do not know where we started, it is difficult to see how far we have progressed!

The notion of progress from baseline also takes some of the pressure off of total goal-attainment. For example, you may set a goal of doing 15 sit-ups in one minute. Your baseline is, say, 7. You practice for one month and are then able to do 12 sit-ups in one minute. The baseline approach would *stress the improvement* from 7 to 12, not the shortfall from 12 from 15. For some kids this is critical.

In goal-setting programs, it is quite natural to focus on goal-attainment. But this should not preclude us from giving ourselves the recognition we deserve for our progress prior to goal-attainment. To use a baseline measurement is to focus on the *process* of attaining goals.

Feedback

Effective feedback is a powerful tool in all teaching/learning situations. Research has shown that feedback is one of the most important factors in learning and growth. The purpose of feedback is to communicate information to the student. This information concerns itself with the student's actions as they relate to his goals.

Feedback operates much like the electronic signals in a guided missile system. It points out actions that are not functional for goal-attainment, and reinforces or commits to memory those actions which are goal-furthering. In other words, feedback helps us keep on target. There are two types of feedback: positive and negative.

Positive feedback communicates to the student that he is improving. It is the proverbial pat on the back. Positive feedback is reinforcing and tends to increase the probability for further improvement. When someone is learning, it is important to inform them when they are doing well, and it is important to also tell them *why* they are doing well.

Negative feedback, on the other hand, concerns itself with mistakes, judgment problems and poor performance. It is usually a necessary part of every teaching/learning situation. In our guided missile analogy, negative feedback keeps the missile on track and oriented toward its goal. Although it is called negative feedback, the results should be productive and goal-enhancing.

Giving negative feedback in an effective way is not always easy. Here are some basic guidelines.

Be Constructive, not destructive

Recognize the positive aspects of the student's effort and suggest concrete steps for improvement. Feedback that destroys confidence or threatens the student is not conducive to learning.

Be specific, not general

When trying to correct a mistake or change a behaviour pattern, be as specific and accurate as possible. Talk in terms of the smallest basic units, not in terms of everything.

Focus on the behaviour, not the person

Give feedback on what a person does, not on what you imagine he is. Speak in terms of a student "acting as if...", or "behaving like...". This leaves the door open for intentional change and avoids threatening personal evaluations.

Direct feedback at changeable behaviour

Focus on immediate, improvable behaviour. Do not criticize things that the student cannot change.

Be sensitive to the timing of feedback

Sometimes timing is everything. There is a time and a place to highlight and correct someone's mistake. Pick appropriate times and settings for feedback sessions.

Always check out feedback for clarity and understanding
Ensure clear communication. Ask students to paraphrase your
feedback. See if they understand what is *wrong* and what must be
done to make it *right*.

A Word about Mistakes

We all know that making mistakes is a natural part of the
learning process. And no one makes mistakes on purpose.

Mistakes can present us with unique learning experiences,
providing us with knowledge that we could never learn without
making them. As one famous statesman once remarked, "We
learn more from our mistakes than from our successes". The
purpose of negative feedback is to turn mistakes or so-called
failure.

Feedback and Baselining

As a tool, feedback can be made more effective if it is coupled with
the practice of baselining. Armed with a baseline measurement, the
Instructor can focus his feedback directly on progress and
improvement. In many situations, this has the effect of turning
negative feedback into positive feedback! The Instructor can couch
his feedback in terms of "You are getting *better*, remember when you
started?" or, "That was better than before, now let's try this..."
Chances for positive feedback are enhanced by the use of baseline
measurements.

Goal-Setting for Youth Groups

What is a Goal?

A goal is a basic unit of program design. It is a desired future state of affairs. It is a statement of intent, connecting a future vision with present realities.

A goal differs from a vision or a dream in that, properly constructed, a goal is subject to some form of measurement to determine whether it has been achieved.

The Art of Purposeful Action

Goals play a key role in the distilling of visions into programs. First, there is a vision. From the vision we can identify a goal. The attainment of a goal is what makes things challenging, and the exact nature of the challenge makes up a tangible program.

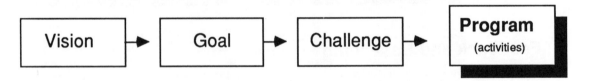

To a certain extent goals are part of the vision, but they also represent the first step in the process of achieving the vision. *Goals make action purposeful.* Goals allow us to focus our energy, and play an important role in helping us get what we want.

In a youth program, goals help in the creation of a group identity. Goals help give each individual member's actions meaning in terms of the whole team. They also provide the group with a sense of worth.

Operational Goals

Goals that are stated in clear and measurable terms are called *operational goals*. They are stated in such a way that we can work with them; they give us a base from which to operate. An operational goal should specify the following:

1) What concrete actions are necessary to signify goal achievement.
2) A time frame for goal achievement.
3) Any special conditions required in the process of attaining the goal.

When dealing with goals (especially group goals), ask yourself, "Is this goal clearly stated, can we tell when it has been achieved, does it have a time frame, and are there any special conditions attached"? The more operational the goal, the easier it is to make a concrete plan of action.

The distinction between operational and non-operational goals can be drawn according to whether a basis exists for relating the goal to possible action by the group.

For example:

Non-operational goal-statement: *"We want to get into dancing"*.

Operational goal-statement: *"We want to start our own teen dance troupe and perform in a show at the Senior's Centre at Christmas time"*.

Both of these statements may conjure up the same vision, but the operationalized goal-statement provides us with important clues about how to proceed.

Long-range goals are often non-operational. They can be broken down into sub-goals that are more operational. Many world-famous athletes, businessmen, and adventurers use this technique to achieve the 'impossible'.

Group Goals and Individual Commitment

When creating (or *negotiating*) group goals, one of the main objectives is to secure maximum individual commitment. The more the group members are commited to the goal, the more likely it is to be achieved, and the more likely it is that each member will get what they wanted. Individual commitment to a group goal depends upon the following factors:

1) How attractive or desirable the goal seems.
2) How likely the group is to accomplish the goal.
3) How challenging the goal is.
4) Being able to tell when the goal has been achieved.
5) Ways in which the group members interact.
6) How much input or control is allowed for each group member.

All these factors should be taken into consideration when group goals are being discussed. A word of caution: a majority vote is not always the best way to resolve disputes about group goals.

A final word about group goals. *Goals are meant to serve the group* and its members. When pursuing a group goal, get feedback from the individual members. Ask them, "Is this what you wanted"? Make sure that the goal is in fact serving the group, and not the group serving the goal!

V: *Theoretical Tools*

Frameworks for Motivation

Motivation can be defined as 'the will to achieve'. It is that which moves a person to act. Motivation gives a program its energy.

Motivating kids is a constant concern in youth programming. We must motivate kids both to become involved and to stay involved. The central question is "What causes kids to become active"? How we answer this question has a major bearing on how we set up and run our programs.

It seems obvious that different things motivate different people. In normal programming situations, the things that motivate kids fall into four progressive categories or stages. These stages can be fit into a framework in order to relate them to the running of youth programs (see Figure V.1).

Stages of Motivation

A motivational stage is determined by two factors: its locus (source), and its time-line.

In stage one the locus of the motivation is *external* to the individual and the time-line is *immediate*. For example, a child does a chore and receives money from his parents when the chore is completed. The reward (money) is immediate and comes from a source external to the person performing the action. This is the simplest level of motivation.

Motivation proceeds in stages until it reaches stage four. Stage four motivation is represented by a self-directed child. He is *internally motivated* and has developed the ability to act in terms of *deferred* or long-term goals.

As a tool, this framework can be useful in two important ways. First, it can be used to help assess the current level of motivation that is most common in a particular youth group. It can help figure out where the group 'is at'. Secondly, it highlights the fact that motivation can be conceived of in progressive stages, with simpler forms of motivation followed by more complex forms. In other words, there is a progression of motivational stages that can be incorporated into the development of a youth program. For example, if your programs were relying predominently on stage two-type motivation (a trophy, for example), then the next stage 'up' would be a program that incorporated stage three-type motivation (a short-term, self-motivated program).

	LOCUS	TIME
Stage 1 ....◀▐▐▐▶	*EXTERNAL* Example: Child does a task for money	*IMMEDIATE*
Stage 2 ....◀▐▐▐▶	*EXTERNAL* Example: Child plays games well to win trophy	*DEFERRED*
Stage 3 ....◀▐▐▐▶	*INTERNAL* Example: Child plays guitar for personal pleasure	*IMMEDIATE*
Stage 4 ....◀▐▐▐▶	*INTERNAL* Example: Child pursues vision of playing in a band	*DEFERRED*

Figure V.1: Achieving Motivation through the Challenge Program

Ideally, the progression would eventually lead to a self-directed youth, pursuing long-term, personal goals. Stage four-type motivation is implicit in the NYC vision. To attain this vision, we use three complementary tools to motivate kids (or, more accurately to help kids motivate themselves). These tools can be used separately, but are most effective when used together in a framework.

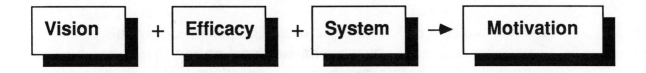

Vision + **Efficacy** + **System** → **Motivation**

Motivating Through Visions

Visions are powerful motivators. Young people are always dreaming of some future state. They *imagine* themselves in certain future-oriented situations. A child may dream of becoming a great dancer, guitar-player or mountain-climber. This dream constitutes an idea of *what he can become*. It is a vision of personal excellence. Everybody has one (at least one), although some people hide their dream or deny its existence all together. But just as every acorn holds within it the makings of a great oak tree, every person holds within himself a vision of personal excellence.

A vision is a series of mental pictures. The person doing the visualizing commonly pictures himself performing in a very competent, often heroic, manner *doing something that he really wants to do.* Implicit in this vision is the will to achieve.

Contained within a vision, there are a number of *images*. These images are more specific than visions. Images are fairly clear and precise. For example, a child's *vision* may be to become a great dancer. The *images* contained in the vision could be those of the child dancing a particular routine in a specific theatre.

The important thing to note about images is that they are very close to taking the form of *goal-statements*. Because images are concrete and specific, they lend themselves to becoming operationalized as goal-statements.

The net effect is to bring a vision 'down' to a series of images, 'down' still further to an operationalized goal-statement.

In youth programs, we can help kids connect themselves with their own visions of personal excellence. We can help kids work through their vision and images to the point where they are able to articulate personal goal-statements. This process goes a long way in helping kids to answer the question, "What do you want to do"? Armed with well-thought-out goal statements, kids are then able to *focus their energy* on achieving what they want. This, in turn, can act as a powerful motivator in itself.

Sometimes more is needed. *Vision-shaping* can help to create a disposition to act, but more may be needed to push this disposition into real action. There are two more tools that can be used to precipitate action.

Motivating Through

Efficacy can be defined as the power to produce effects or intended results. *A sense of personal efficacy* refers to a person's belief that the results of his actions match his intention. It is a feeling that he can achieve his goals. It is a general feeling; a feeling that goals are meant to be achieved and that he has the wherewithal to achieve them.

Some people call this a sense of 'can do', or a 'winning feeling'. It does not have to relate to any goal in particular, just to a person's goals in general. This positive (yet realistic) attitude is a necessary component in the motivation equation. For without the belief that he can act to achieve his goals (intentions), a person cannot motivate himself.

To promote a sense of personal efficacy in a child(ren), several guidelines can be followed:

Start small. Have the child articulate even his smallest intentions (like going to school tomorrow, or playing floor hockey after school). Have him write it down. Help the child become conscious of all the intentions that he turns into actions and accomplishments. Turn intentions into goal-statements. Pace the growth of goals to the child's ability to achieve them.

Use feedback skillfully. Take advantage of all opportunities to use positive feedback. Use baseline measurements to establish a theme of improvement. Use a positive reinforcement schedule. Begin by reinforcing all goal-furthering actions, and later reinforce only the most effective behaviours. This stimulates the child to reach forward and perform at his highest level of effectiveness.

Believe in kids. Certainly one of the most important factors in the creation of a child's sense of efficacy is the Instructor's belief in him. When an Instructor expresses a sincere belief in the child's ability to achieve his goals, then the child's feelings about himself are also enhanced. As Instructors we must believe in what children can become.

Motivating Through 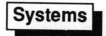 Systems

A child's sense of personal efficacy is greatly enhanced by the use of *systems*. Combined with visions and efficacy, systems can round out the motivation equation.

A system is an integrated plan. It is a step-by-step process that is focused on goal achievement. Working systematically toward a goal means using a system that takes all variables into account. Through a system, actions are laid out in a logical sequence, and *effort can be related directly to results*. When the actions needed to achieve a goal are laid out systematically and the path is clear, then motivation is enhanced. It has been our experience that working towards visions is best accomplished systematically.

The action contract on page 28 is a system. It lays out action in an integrated, step-by-step approach. The format of challenge courses (i.e., Challenge Event, Study Units and Practical Units) also represents a system.

Motivation is a complex psychological phenomenon, and yet it is a major part of our jobs as youth care workers. There is a limit to what we can/should do to motivate kids. We can work toward removing the obstacles to motivation. We can do this by helping kids *visualize* their goals, develop a sense of personal *efficacy*, and develop *systems* for effective action. After that, it's up to them.

Self-Esteem

What is Self-Esteem?

As youth care workers, we frequently come across the term *self-esteem*. Many times we are asked to help a child raise his self-esteem, or we are told that so-and-so has a low self-esteem.

The notion of self-esteem has been criticized of late because of its vagueness, and the difficulties encountered when attempting to measure changes. How can we tell if a child's self-esteem is on the rise? It is even difficult to come up with a precise definition to work with.

We do know that the word *esteem* means to value or to estimate the worth of. So *self-esteem* must refer to the value or worth that one psychologically assigns to oneself. Although this definition is still vague, it can be worked with in the following manner.

Self-Esteem and Efficacy

A child's sense of worth is, to a large extent, dependent on the achievement of personal goals. What is just as important is the generalized feeling that personal goals can be achieved. In short, self-esteem is directly related to a sense of personal efficacy.

If a child's past is full of broken dreams and thwarted intention, then he is likely to place a low value on himself as a person. On the other hand, those children who are successful in the pursuit of their personal goals are likely to place a higher value on themselves as people. And the children that believe that, in general, their personal goals can be achieved are likely to experience a greater sense of *worth*.

Raising Self-Esteem

As youth care workers, we can help children create their own visions of personal excellence. This step alone can go a long way to raising a child's self esteem. They learn to value themselves by valueing their visions. But this step by itself may not be sufficient.

We can also play an important part in helping to make children's visions become real. The bulk of this manual has been written to help youth care workers teach children systems for effective action. Using challenge courses, clubs, or action contracts, children can learn to be effective in the pursuit of their goals.

In terms of self-esteem, our main objective is to help children align their *intentions* (goals) with their *behaviour* (actions). A child's sense of worth increases to the extent that he becomes a person who *can do* what he wants (intends) to do. Matching his behaviour with his intentions increases the control he has over his own life.

Frequently children with low self-esteem feel that they have little or no control over the course of their lives. They feel that they are at the mercy of outside forces, and therefore they do not take responsibility for what happens to them. This can set up a vicious cycle of failure and plummeting self-worth.

NYC programs can help change this. Setting and achieving personal goals naturally makes children aware of the control they can have over their own lives. These children begin to realize that they can achieve what they want to set out for themselves. From there, they experience a greater sense of worth, and begin to search for goals that are worthy of them.

VI: *Proven Programs and Ideas*

Backpacking

Challenge Event

> Three-Day Backpacking/Camping Trip

Practical Units

> Planning Meeting
> Food Purchase
> Check Clothing

> Day Hike
> Survival Practice

Study Units

Maps and Compass	Outdoor Clothing	Shelters and Shelter-Building	Safety and Survival

Lesson Plans

– How to Read a Map – How to Use a Compass – Stove-Lighting	– Nutrition – Menu-Planning – Ropes and Knots	– How to Set Up Tents – Making a Lean-To – Safety Techniques	– Hypothermia – Getting Lost

Challenge Category: Adventure

Designer: Steve Musson

Bicycle Touring

Challenge Event

> Plan and Participate in 3-Day Bicycle Touring Trip

Practical Units

Planning Meeting		Series of Practice and Day Rides

Study Units

Bicycle Repair and Maintenance	Traffic Safety	Equipment for Touring	Long-Distance Cycling Techniques

Lesson Plans

Bicycle Repair and Maintenance	Traffic Safety	Equipment for Touring	Long-Distance Cycling Techniques
- Clean Chain/ Sprockets	- Safety Standards	- Clothing	- Nutrition
- Gear Adjustment	- Safe Riding Practices	- Panniers	- Physiology
- Tire Repair	- Accident Prevention	- Camping Gear	- Pedalling Techniques

Challenge Category: **Adventure**

Designer: **Steve Musson**

Downhill Skiing

Challenge Event

> Planning + Participating in 2-Day Ski Holiday

Practical Units

Day Trip to Local Mountain		Tour of Ski Shop Equipment/ Clothes/ Mechanics

Study Units

Fund-Raising	Skiing as a Sport	Ski Training Theory	Fitness for Skiers

Lesson Plans

Fund-Raising	Skiing as a Sport	Ski Training Theory	Fitness for Skiers
– Goals	– History	– How to Train	– Stretching
– Methods	– Popularity	– Ability Evaluation	– Cardio-vascular Fitness
– Events	– What do you need to Participate?	– Snow Plow – Stem Christie	– Exercises – Balance and Control

Challenge Category: **Adventure**

Designer: **Bill Saul**

Puppet Troupe

Challenge Event		Creating a Puppet Troupe (Hand Puppets)	

Practical Units	Performing		Technical

Study Units	The History	The Puppets	The Creation	The Production

Lesson Plans	— Original Purposes of Puppets — Varieties of Staging	— Manipulation — Characterization — Voice Quality — Movement	— Finding and Adapting Script — Building Puppet Theatre — Making Puppets — Costuming — Organization — Sets	— Publicity — Casts — Finding Locations — Art of Approaching Prospective Hosts

Challenge Category:	*Designer:*
Creative Expression	Kate Quenville

Rock Video

	Challenge Event		
Challenge Event		Making a Rock Video (Performing Program)	

Challenge Event

> Making a Rock Video (Performing Program)

Practical Units

Lip Synch		Photo Session

Study Units

Drama	Dance	Modelling	Fashion Coordination

Lesson Plans

– Acting	– Music	– Posture	– Colours
– Stage Presence	– Rhythm	– Walking	– Make-Up
– Voice	– Coordination	– How to be Photographed	– Hair
– Movement	– Movement	– Camera Work	– Fashion/ Style
– Self-Awareness	– Choreography		– Image

Challenge Category: **Creative Expression**

Designer: **Kate Quenville**

Rock Video

	Challenge Event		
Challenge Event		Making a Rock Video (Technical Program)	

Challenge Event

> Making a Rock Video (Technical Program)

Practical Units

> Filming a Lip Synch Contest

> Shooting a Photo Session

Study Units

The Video Camera	The Art of Filming	The S.L.R. Camera	The Art of Photography

Lesson Plans

— Mechanics Theory	— Angles	— Types of Cameras	— Angles
— How it Works	— Lighting	— How it Works	— Lighting
— Maintenance	— Editing	— Mechanical Theory	— Filters' special Effects
— Types of Cameras	— Special Effects	— Maintenance	— Developing
— Practical Use		— Practical Use	— Printing

Challenge Category:	Designer:
Creative Expression	Kate Quenville

T-Shirt Design Contest

Challenge Event

Setting-up + Participating in T-Shirt Design Contest

Practical Units

Block Printing Wall Hanging	Tie Dye or Stencil Pillowcase	Batik Hanging

Study Units

Block Printing	Tie Dye	Fabric Stencilling	Batik

Lesson Plans

— History	— History	— History	— History
— Method	— Method	— Method	— Method
— Sample	— Sample	— Sample	— Sample

Challenge Category: Creative Expression

Designer: Heather Kennedy

Art Club

	Challenge Event
Challenge Event	Art Exhibit by the Club

Practical Units

Artistic Creations		"Let's Get this Show on The Road"

Study Units

Painting Watercolours	Sculpture Clay	Structural Set-Up	Public Relations

Lesson Plans

Painting Watercolours	Sculpture Clay	Structural Set-Up	Public Relations
— Line	— Pinch Methods	— Communication	— Skills
— Form	— Coil Method	— Choosing an Appropriate Facility	— Advertising
— Space	— Slab Method		— What Is It?
— Colour	— Sculpture Method	— Covering Costs	— Donations?
— Texture		— Display Method	— Tactics / Target Group
— Choosing a Subject	— Wire Frame Method	— Set-Up (Acquiring/ Making Display Methods)	— Duties of the Curator
— Framing	— Firing		
	— Glazing		

Challenge Category:	Designer:
Creative Expression	Carrie Froese

Soccer Challenge

Challenge Event

> Challenge Cup Game
> Students vs. Semi-pros

Practical Units

> Watching Top Calibre PCL Game

> Student Tournament in World Cup Format

Study Units

Rules of Soccer	Films of World Class Players	Fitness	Skills

Lesson Plans

— Reasons for Rules	— Analysis — Motivation	— Endurance — Coordination — Circuit Training — Exercises: Isometric Isotonic	— Shooting — Heading — Passing — Trapping — Dribbling — Position Play — Goaltending

Challenge Category: *Sports*

Designer: *Randy Wallis*

Hockey Challenge

Challenge Event

Organize
Participation
Cosum Hockey
Tournament

Practical Units

| Watch Vancouver Canucks Practice | Organize Cosum Hockey League | "Showdown" and Accuracy Competition |

Study Units

| Hockey Fundamentals | Hockey Strategies | Hockey Rules | Video Analysis |

Lesson Plans

Hockey Fundamentals	Hockey Strategies	Hockey Rules	Video Analysis
– Stick Control	– Offense	– Refereeing	– View Video
– Passing	– Defense	– Penalties	– Note Fundamentals
– Note strategies	– Shooting	– Passing Plays	– Scorekeeping
– Goal Tending	– Power Plays	– Basic Rules	– Note Rules

Challenge Category:	Designer:
Sports	**Bill Saul**

Wrestling

Challenge Event

Formation of Wrestling Club *

* To compete with other Groups in the City

Practical Units

Watch Wrestling Tournament at University		Wrestling Tournament Within Clubs

Study Units

History of Wrestling	Wrestling Today	Physical Endurance	Basic Holds and Moves

Lesson Plans

– Greco-Roman	– Olympic	– Stretching	– Coordination
– History / Olympic Wrestling	– Local Wrestling scene	– Cardio-vascular	– Discipline
	– Falsity of Pro Wrestling	– Muscular Development	– Takedowns
– Other Forms	– Variations	– Wrestling Exercises	– Recoveries

Challenge Category:	Designer:
Sports	Bill Saul

Fun Fitness and Your Body

Challenge Event

> Formation of a Fitness Club

Practical Units

> Fun Fitness Club

> Experiments and Games

Study Units

Muscle/ Strength	Aerobics	Your Body	Nutrition

Lesson Plans

— Muscles	— Heart	— Skin	— Food Groups
— Joints	— Lungs	— Bones	— What we Need

Challenge Category:
Sports

Designer:
Barb Waterman

First Aid (Attainment of 'Staying Alive')

Challenge Event

Basic Competency in First Aid Emergencies

Practical Units

Emergency Simulation and Practice

First Aid and Student Evaluation

Study Units

Handling an Emergency	Breathing Emergencies	Bleeding Emergencies	Care for Shock

Lesson Plans

— Response	— Artificial Respiration	— Bandaging	— Causes of Shock
— Priorities	— Obstructed Airway	— External Bleeding	— Treatment
— Obtaining Help		— Internal Bleeding	— Accident Prevention

Challenge Category:
Practical Skills

Designer:
Steve Musson (Red Cross)

Gardening

Challenge Event		Garden in a Box	

Practical Units	Making a Flower Box		Field Trip to a Garden Shop

Study Units	Design of the Flower Box	Construction of the Flower Box	Horticulture: Flowers/ Veggies	Soil and Material
Lesson Plans	— Wood: Types and Kinds — Draw out Design — Out-trip to Buy Supplies	— Safety in Woodwork — Area — Cutting of Wood	— Horticultural Botanical Gardening — What will grow in limited areas — Organic — Different Flowers and Arrangements	— Garden Care — Weed Control — Organic Insect Control — Seeds and Seedlings

Challenge Category: **Practical Skills**

Designer:

Chess Tournament

Challenge Event

> Enter a Chess Tournament

Practical Units

> Analyze Games of World Champs

> Play a Chess Master

Study Units

Rules of Chess	Chess Notation	Opening and Middle Games	End Games

Lesson Plans

— Movement of Pieces		— Queen Gambit	— End Game
— Chessboard		— Ruy Lopez	— Composition
— Special Moves		— Giuoco Piano	— King and Pawn vs. King

Challenge Category: Logical Inquiry

Designer: Randy Watlis

Travel

	Challenge Event	
Challenge Event		Formation of a Travel Club

Challenge Event

> Formation of a Travel Club

Practical Units

Visit a Travel Bureau		Plan an Imaginary Trip

Study Units

Destination	Transportation	Research	Financial

Lesson Plans

– Choosing Where to Go	– Safety	– Itinerary	– Cost of Transport
– Interests	– Type of Transportation	– Resources	– Fundraising
	– Time-Factors	– Weather	– Realistic Goals
			– Currencies

Challenge Category: *Logical Inquiry*

Designer: *Barb Waterman*

Astronomy

Challenge Event	Star Identification on Sleep Out	

Practical Units

Make a Telescope		Design a Model Solar System

Study Units

Stars and Zodiac	Man and Sun	Planets	The Solar System

Lesson Plans

Stars and Zodiac	Man and Sun	Planets	The Solar System
- Constellations	- Distances	- Earth	- Formation
- Distances	- Energy	- Other Planets	- Gravity
- Astronomy Symbols	- Eclipses, etc.	- Meteors, etc.	- Our Solar System

Challenge Category:	Designer:
Logical Inquiry	Barb Waterman

Kids and Seniors

Challenge Event

> Befriending Seniors on a Long-Term Basis

Practical Units

Visit a Senior Facility		All-Day Activity — children/ seniors

Study Units

What is a Senior?	Activities	Games	Interacting with Seniors

Lesson Plans

- Characteristics	- Letterwriting	- What Seniors Enjoy	- Sharing
- Common Ailments	- Shopping	- Crib, Dominoes	- Learning
- Needs	- Reading		
	- Sewing, Handicrafts	- Bingo, Checkers	

Challenge Category: *Community Service*

Designer: *Barb Waterman*

Recycling Program

Challenge Event

> Set-Up and Run a Recycling Program

Practical Units

Visit a Recycling Plant		Advertise and Promote Recycling Program

Study Units

Ecology	Location	Advertising	Administration

Lesson Plans

Ecology	Location	Advertising	Administration
— Why Recycle?	— Where to Recycle	— Advertising Methods	— Budget
— What to Recycle	— Community Awareness	— Costs	— Management Objectives
— How to Recycle	— Research	— A Coordinated Strategy	— Logistics
	— Permission		

Challenge Category:	Designer:
Community Service	Barb Waterman

Volunteers

Challenge Event

Formation of a Volunteer Bureau

Practical Units

25 Hours of Volunteer Service

Design
- Application
- Information Card
- Set Up Referral Service

Study Units

Volunteerism	Identification	Research	Administration

Lesson Plans

Volunteerism	Identification	Research	Administration
– What is a Volunteer?	– Positions	– Information needed	– Training
– Why you?	– Abilities	– Referral System	– Job Cards
– Commitment	– Needs	– Agencies	– Advertising
– Realistic Goals	– Suitability	– Volunteers	– Evaluation
	– What do I get?	– Where/How?	
	– What can I offer?		

Challenge Category: Community Service

Designer: Barb Waterman

Daycare Aide

Challenge Event

> To Be a Daycare Junior Aide

Practical Units

> Visit a Daycare Centre

> Practical Experience in a Daycare Centre

Study Units

Good Work Ethics Reference	Safety Awareness Centre + Procedure	Guiding . Supervision	Activities for Young Children Play

Lesson Plans

- Responsibilities of an Employee	- Importance of Centre Safety	- Personal Care for Children	- The Importance of Play
- Modelling good Personal + Health Habits	- Purpose of the Centre	- Communicating with Children	- Using Resource Material to Plan an Activity
- Punctuality	- Routine and Requirements	- Guiding Behaviour	- Working with an Individual Child
- Appearance		- Helping the Child	
- Follow Directions			
- Asking Questions			
- Enthusiasm			
- Job Description			
- Evaluation			

Challenge Category: Job Experience

Designer: Joanne Ouellette

Babysitting Certification

Challenge Event

> Babysitting Certification Competency in Child Care + Safety

Practical Units

> Practicum

> Babysitting Test and Student Evaluation

Study Units

> Basic Child Care

> First Aid Priorities

> Child Safety

> Child Behaviour

Lesson Plans

Basic Child Care	First Aid Priorities	Child Safety	Child Behaviour
– Changing	– Care for Shock	– Accident Prevention	– Dealing with children
– Holding	– Treating Injuries	– Safety Tips	– Creative play
– Feeding	– Artificial Respiration	– Safety in Toys	– Discipline
– Bathing	– Choking	– House Safety	– Developmental Activities
– Bed	– Burns, Bumps		
– Crying	– Falls		
	– Cuts + Poisons		
	– Dealing with Fires		

Challenge Category: Job Experience

Designer: Kate Quenville

Youth Power Office

Challenge Event

> Formation and Running of Youth Power Office

Practical Units

> Phone Answering Service

> Interviewing Management

Study Units

Good Work Ethics	Phone Answering Techniques	Jobs	Budget Management

Lesson Plans

– Punctuality	– Types of Phones	– Job Description	– Budget
– Appearance			– Wages
– Enthusiasm	– Courtesy	– Suitability	– Responsibility
– Evaluation	– Message-Taking	– Job Search	

Challenge Category: *Job Experience*

Designer: *Barb Waterman*

Feelin' Good

Challenge Event

To Feel Good
With Your
Own Personal
Health and
Fitness Program

Practical Units

Practicing Good Eating Habits + Nutrition/ Visit Health Food Store		Fitness Classes + Jogging

Study Units

Life Style Awareness	Weight Control	Fitness Is ...	Flexibility . Strength/ Endurance

Lesson Plans

— Your Life Style Today	— Nutritional Analysis	— What Fitness Means To You	— Muscular Strength and Endurance
— Eating Habits	— Diets / Fads	— Setting Realistic Goals	— Flexibility
— Exercise	— Health Food Requirements	— Core Exercises	— Aerobics/ Jogging
— Intensity	— Setting Realistic Goals		

Challenge Category:	Designer:
Personal Improvement	Barb Waterman

More Ideas for New Youth Challenge Programs

Adventure

Travel club
Outdoor games group
Mountaineering course
Sailing trip

Creative Expression

Theatre group
Writer's club
Photography club
Journalism course

Sports

Ski challenge
Windsurfing club
Rugby team

Practical Skills

C.P.R. course
Woodworking group
International cooking class
Fashion coordination course

Logical Inquiry

Personal finance course
Inventor's club
Parliamentarian's club
Mind expanders

Community Service

School patrol group
Library aide program
Fund-raising committee

Job Experience

Stockroom assistant course
Pet exercise service
Babysitter referral service

Personal Improvement

Memory training course
Problem-solving course
Goal-setting club

A Final Word

School-age child care workers are on the verge of something exciting. Our role in the development of children is expanding. Opportunities to make a real difference in someone's life are increasing all the time. But to be effective in our new role it is necessary to develop an integrated approach to youth care. We must be able to see clearly that toward which we strive. Our methods must be systematic and visionary.

If we can help our kids reach forward to the difficult but valuable achievements that they desire, then we have done our job. If we can work to allow our programs to become vehicles for children's self-direction, then we have exceeded that which is expected of us. The quest for quality youth programs is never-ending.

We welcome any suggestions or ideas from you, the reader. Please write to:

The New Youth Challenge:

School Age NOTES
P.O. Box 120674
Nashville, TN.
U.S.A.   37212
Telephone: (615) 292-4957

Challenge Education Associates
3284 Tennyson Crescent,
North Vancouver, B.C.
Canada   V7K 2A8
Telephone: (604) 980-1737

About the Authors

Maurice Gibbons, a professor emeritus in the Faculty of Education at Simon Fraser University, is a Harvard-trained specialist in program development. He has taught in elementary and secondary schools and has written several books and numerous articles on how people educate themselves. His best known works are "Walkabout: Searching for the Right Passage from Childhood and School" (*The Kappan* May, 1974) and *The New Secondary Education*. Maurice is also an accomplished wood sculptor whose work has exhibited in Vancouver, San Francisco, New York and Australia.

Steve Musson has been working with youth groups since 1978. He has developed and taught basic rock-climbing, whitewater canoeing, backpacking and other challenging programs for young people. He has worked with kids in Outdoor Education, summer camps, leadership training and school-aged child care facilities. He is a skilled outdoorsman who regularly challenges himself. Steve is currently an area manager for the Boys and Girls Club and continues his work in providing innovative programs for school-age child care.

ISBN 0-917505-02-6

Selected Bibliography

Branden, Nathaniel. *The Psychology of Self-Esteem.*
　　Toronto: Bantam Books, 1969.

Gibbons, Maurice and Norman, Peter. *Self-Directed Action.*
　　North Vancouver: Challenge Education Associates, 1983.

Johnson, D.W. and Johnson, F.P. *Joining Together: Group Theory &*
　　Group Skills. New Jersey: Prentice-Hall, 1975.

Sher, Barbara. *Wishcraft: How to Get What You Want.*
　　New York: Ballantine Books, 1979.

Simon, Sidney et al. *Values Clarification.*
　　New York: Dodd, Mead and Co., 1972.